The Cherokee

An Independent Nation

by Anne M. Todd

Consultants:

Myrtle Driver Johnson
Cultural-Traditional Specialist
Eastern Band of the Cherokee Nation
North Carolina

Garfield Long
Linguist
Eastern Band of the
Cherokee Nation
North Carolina

Lisa Stopp
Literature Review Coordinator
Cherokee Nation
Oklahoma

Bridgestone Books

an imprint of Capstone Press
Mankato, Minnesota

Bridgestone Books are published by Capstone Press
151 Good Counsel Drive, P.O. Box 669, Mankato, Minnesota 56002
http://www.capstone-press.com

Printed in the United States of America.
Library of Congress Cataloging-in-Publication Data
Todd, Anne M.
    Cherokee: an independent nation/by Anne M. Todd.
        v. cm.—(American Indian nations)
    Includes bibliographical references and index.
    Contents: The Cherokee—Life among the Cherokee—Conflicts and
    culture—Life in a modern world—Sharing the old ways.
    ISBN 0-7368-1355-1 (hardcover)
    1. Cherokee Indians—History—Juvenile literature. 2. Cherokee
    Indians—Social life and customs—Juvenile literature. [1. Cherokee
    Indians. 2. Indians of North America--Southern states.] I. Title.
    II. American Indian Nations series.
    E99.C5 T66 2003
    975.004'9755—dc21   2002002653

Editorial Credits
Bradley P. Hoehn, editor; Kia Adams, designer and illustrator; Wanda Winch,
photo researcher; Karen Risch, product planning editor

Photo Credits
Kit Breen, cover, 11; Marilyn "Angel" Wynn, cover inset, 6, 10, 16 (both photos),
32, 45; Unicorn Stock Photos/Jeff Greenberg, 4; Visuals Unlimited/Charles
McRae, 8; PhotoDisc, Inc.,12-13; Capstone Press/Gary Sundermeyer, 13;
Cherokee Historical Association, 15, 18, 41, 43; Architect of the Capitol/William
H. Powell, 20; North Wind Picture Archives, 22, 29 (top), 44; Annenberg Rare
Book and Manuscript Library, University of Pennsylvania, 24; Woolaroc
Museum, Bartlesville, OK/Robert L. Lindneux, 28; Stock Montage, Inc./The
Newberry Library, 29 (bottom); Charlie Soap, 34; The Cherokee Nation, 30, 33,
Sammy Still, 36; Guthrie Studios/John Guthrie, 38

2 3 4 5 6 07 06 05 04 03

Table of Contents

Features

Cherokee gather together to take part in cultural events to celebrate their heritage and culture. The Cherokee above were attending such an event.

Chapter One

The Cherokee

The Cherokee are a group of American Indians who live mostly in North Carolina and Oklahoma. They call themselves the Ani-Yun'wiya, which means "principal people." They make up the second largest Indian nation living in the United States today. The U.S. government identifies more than 240,000 people as Cherokee. More than 730,000 people classify themselves as Cherokee.

Three Nations of Cherokee

The United States government recognizes three Cherokee groups. The Cherokee Nation and the United Keetoowah Band of Cherokee Indians (UKB) are based in Oklahoma. The Eastern Band of Cherokee Indians have headquarters in North Carolina.

Unlike many other American Indians, Cherokee do not live on reservations. Some American Indians live on land set aside for them by the U.S. government. But the Cherokee live in rural towns and urban cities across the United States. Many members of the Cherokee Nation live in northeastern Oklahoma in a 14-county area controlled by the tribe. Tahlequah, a town located within these 14 counties, is the capital of the Cherokee Nation.

The United Keetoowah Band (UKB) of Cherokee Indians live in the same 14 counties in northeastern Oklahoma as the Cherokee Nation. The UKB are working with the U.S. government to establish reservations of their own.

The Eastern Band of Cherokee live on land covering five counties in western North Carolina. These Cherokees still live on the land their ancestors did.

This is the seal of the Cherokee Nation.

UNITED STATES

OKLAHOMA

NORTH CAROLINA

ATLANTIC OCEAN

Gulf of Mexico

N

W *E*

S

PACIFIC OCEAN

Legend

Cherokee Nation and United Keetoowah Band (UKB)

Eastern Band of Cherokee

The Cherokee came from an area of the Appalachian Mountains. These mountains are located in the Southeastern United States.

Chapter Two

Life among the Cherokee

Before contact with Europeans, the Cherokee people lived in the southern Appalachian Mountains. To the Cherokee, this area was known as the "land of the blue mist," or "sha-cona-ge." This area included the present-day states of Georgia, Alabama, North Carolina, South Carolina, Tennessee, Kentucky, West Virginia, and Virginia. The total land area was about 135,000 square miles (349,650 square kilometers).

The Cherokee grew most of the food they ate. Women planted and harvested corn, beans, and squash. They called these foods the "three sisters." Men fished and hunted for game, such as deer and fowl.

The Cherokee lived in towns of 30 to 60 families. In the center of the town, they built a seven-sided council house. It usually was built on a mound. The Cherokee gathered at the

After the 1800s, the Cherokee built their houses out of logs. These homes were warmer and sturdier than their earlier houses.

Cherokee built their winter houses with a circular frame of mud, animal hair, grass, and clay.

council house for ceremonies, town meetings, and celebrations. The Cherokee built their homes around the council house. The council house also was the site of the Sacred Fire. The Cherokee kept the fire burning all year.

Early Cherokee built houses with a circular framework of woven branches covered with mud, animal hair, grass, and clay. The house looked like an upside-down basket. It was partially sunken into the ground. In later years, the Cherokee built log cabins with one door and a hole or chimney in the bark-covered roof for smoke to escape.

Family Roles

Young babies and children stayed close to their mothers. Infants rode in cloth carriers on their mothers' backs. Small children played beside their mothers while they worked.

Cherokee boys trained to become hunters and warriors. Boys worked to improve their coordination and build their strength. They practiced hunting using blowguns. A blowgun is hollow like a straw. A blowgun was used to shoot small game, such as birds or rabbits. Cherokee boys made blowguns from a hollow plant called river cane. They made darts of wood with tips of thistle. A thistle plant has sharp, pricklelike needles. The thistle kept the wooden dart steady as a boy blew it out the hollow river cane. Cherokee boys practiced for hours with blowguns and darts trying to hit a target.

Men hunted deer with bows and arrows and used spears to catch fish. They defended their land and protected their families. The men also built the houses and made tools, weapons, and canoes.

Sv-Ga-Ta (Baked Apples)

Long ago, Cherokees baked native green apples under a covering of hot ashes and live coals. You can bake a similar version of this Native American treat in the oven at home.

Ingredients:

¼ cup (50 mL) brown sugar
¼ cup (50 mL) chopped pecans
¼ teaspoon (1 mL) allspice
4 large apples (Granny Smith, Jonathan or similar baking variety)
4 tablespoons (60 mL) butter

Equipment:

wooden mixing spoon
small mixing bowl
dry-ingredient measuring cups
measuring spoons
paring knife

aluminum foil
baking pan
pot holders
food tongs

What you do:

1. Preheat oven to 350°F (180°C).
2. With wooden spoon, mix together brown sugar, pecans, and allspice in a small bowl.
3. With adult supervision, use the paring knife to make a hole in the center of the apple. Carefully remove the seeds and core without cutting the skin at the bottom of the apple.
4. Enlarge the center hole enough to hold the filling.
5. Place 1 tablespoon (15 mL) butter in each apple hole.
6. Add one-fourth of the filling into each apple.
7. Wrap each apple tightly in aluminum foil. Place wrapped apples top side down in a baking pan.
8. Bake 10 to 15 minutes.
9. With pot holders, remove baking pan from oven.
10. Use tongs to turn apples right-side up. Unwrap and serve.

Makes 4 large or 8 small servings

Cherokee women planted crops, prepared meals, and wove baskets. Cherokee women also took an active role in the Cherokee government. The people elected a clan mother to speak at town meetings on behalf of the women. Some women also became warriors. Girls worked beside their mothers and grandmothers to learn how to sew, cook, and plant.

Cherokee elders helped to raise the children. During ceremonies, the elders told legends, or stories, of times past. Most Cherokee stories include a moral, or lesson in the story.

Cherokee people were very independent in their daily lives. It was typical for the tribe to come together for ceremonies or special events. They would also come together in times of war.

Basketry

Cherokee women and children made baskets to gather, carry, and store food. Some baskets could even be used to hold water. To add color to the baskets, women gathered and boiled plants in water. The women then soaked the wood in the water to absorb the dye. Walnut husks made a brown dye and bloodroot made a red dye. Bloodroot is a type of poppy that has a red root.

One Cherokee woman would make many baskets in her lifetime. They were all hand woven and dyed using natural dyes made from plants.

Stickball

Cherokee men played a game called stickball to help them stay fit and healthy. Stickball teams of 10 to 50 players tried to put a ball made out of deerskin into their opponent's goal. They could touch the ball after picking it up with a special ball stick. It had one small basket on one end for catching and tossing the ball. Today, both men and women play. The women can use their hands if they choose, instead of the ball sticks.

The Cherokee made most of their baskets from white oak, river cane, or honeysuckle strips. They boiled the river cane, honeysuckle, and white oak, and cleaned the strips. Women then wove the wood into a basket. After she finished weaving the basket, the woman would leave it in the sun to dry.

Stomp Dance

The Cherokee have a religious ceremony called the Stomp Dance. It was conducted on a special dance site called the stompground. On the morning of the dance, a firekeeper used an ember from the Sacred Fire to start the new fire for the Stomp Dance. The Sacred Fire burned all year long to represent the nation.

The firekeeper carefully positioned the logs so that one log was pointed in each of the four cardinal directions. They are north, south, east, and west. The Cherokee believed that there were seven directions and added above, below, and center to the directions.

In the morning, men came to prepare for the dance and to give prayer. Women began to prepare a large feast, using special cooking fires. In the afternoon, the Cherokee gathered to listen to stories. They also played games, visited, and ate.

Cherokee people conducted the Eagle Dance to ensure a successful hunt or to cure a sick person. This Eagle Dance was performed in the play *Unto These Hills*.

The dance began at sundown and continued through the next morning. Dancers followed in a line behind the stompground chief or leader. The men and boys sang and everyone danced as they moved around the circle.

Some women and girls were chosen to be shakers. They wore leg rattles made of seven turtle shells filled with pebbles and tied together. Shakers stomped their feet to create a rhythm in which the other participants of the Stomp Dance could dance and sing. The Cherokee still perform the Stomp Dance today.

Eagle Dance and Green Corn Ceremony

The Cherokee Eagle Dance combined many songs and different dances. The dancers dressed like eagles and moved while dancing around a fire. The Cherokee conducted this ceremony to ensure a successful hunt or to cure a sick person.

The Green Corn Ceremony represented the beginning of a new year. It was performed when the corn was ripe. During this ceremony, the Sacred Fire was put out, as were all fires in every home. A Cherokee healer then started a new Sacred Fire to last through the next year. The fires in each of the homes were then lit from the new Sacred Fire.

In 1540, Hernando de Soto arrived in North America. He came with other Spanish explorers to look for gold. He believed the Cherokee people knew where the gold was hidden.

Chapter Three

Conflicts and Culture

In the 1500s, the Cherokee met with European explorers. In 1540, Spanish explorer Hernando de Soto arrived with his soldiers to look for gold. De Soto did not treat the Cherokee kindly because he believed they would not share the locations of the gold mines. He ordered his men to enslave some of the Cherokee. If the Cherokee refused to practice his Christian religion, de Soto had them killed.

The Spanish explorers carried diseases that were new to North America. The Cherokee had no medicines to prevent or cure these new diseases. Smallpox and measles were two of the diseases that killed thousands of Cherokees. From the 1600s through the 1700s these and other diseases carried by the explorers killed about 95 percent of the Americans Indians.

When the British came to Cherokee lands in the 1620s, they were friendly to the Cherokee. In fact, many British men

Cherokee brought beaver skins to the British to trade for pots, pans, beads, rifles, and other items.

married Cherokee women. By 1673, the Cherokee had begun to trade with the British. The British exchanged pots, pans, beads, and rifles for the Cherokee's deerskins and beaver furs.

The French and Indian War

In the late 1600s, French traders came to North America. They competed with the English traders. Both the French and the English wanted control of North America and the profitable fur trade. In 1754, France and Great Britain went to war. In North America this conflict became known as the French and Indian War (1754–1763). Most American Indians sided with the French. A few, like the Cherokee, sided with the British.

But, the Cherokee and British later became enemies during the war. British farmers discovered that a group of starving Cherokee had killed their cows and eaten the meat. This theft caused revenge attacks on both sides. Many Cherokee, French, and British were killed.

In 1759, the British defeated the French in Quebec, Canada. The British took control of the land that France owned. They also took away much of the land the Cherokee controlled.

The United States

In 1783, Americans won their independence from Great Britain and formed the United States of America. The U.S. government wanted peace between whites and American Indians. The government believed the easiest way to achieve this peace was to teach the American Indians to be more like whites.

In 1839, the Cherokee wrote their own constitution creating a government separate from the United States.

Government officials introduced plows and spinning wheels to Cherokees. They hoped to see the Cherokee men farm and the women weave clothes for their families. They also set up schools to teach Cherokee children to read and write in English.

Although the Cherokee people were beginning to take on more similarities with the whites, they also kept their own identity. In 1839, the Cherokee wrote their own constitution. They called themselves the Cherokee Nation. They had a separate government from the United States. The Cherokee constitution provided for a General Council, elected by the people, to rule the Cherokee Nation. The Cherokee people would elect the council. The constitution clearly defined Cherokee lands. These lands included parts of the states of Georgia, Alabama, Tennessee, and North Carolina.

White settlers who lived in the states of Georgia, Alabama, Tennessee, and North Carolina did not agree with the Cherokee constitution's definition of Cherokee land. Settlers found gold on Cherokee land in Georgia. Thousands of gold hunters entered Georgia to look for gold. They demanded that the U.S. government convince the Cherokee to go west and leave their Cherokee homelands.

Trail of Tears

When all of the Cherokee did not leave Georgia and the surrounding area, the government decided to force those who refused to move. Soldiers stormed into hundreds of Cherokee villages and forced men, women, and children to leave their homes. The Cherokee were only allowed to bring what they could carry on their backs. Cherokee who tried to resist leaving their homes were shot and killed.

After the Cherokee left their homes, white people came in and stole Cherokee livestock and burned many homes. The Cherokee would never see these belongings again.

Soldiers gathered together more than 16,000 Cherokee people. The soldiers forced them to walk from Alabama, Georgia, Mississippi, and North Carolina to Oklahoma. The trail crossed through four present-day states. The 800-mile (1,300 kilometers) journey took over six months to complete.

The journey began during a drought. It was a time when there was little water or food. People became sick, but they still had to walk. Some were lucky enough to ride horses. The weather turned colder for the winter, and more people grew sick. Some were sick from disease, others were sick from starvation. More than 4,000 people died on the journey. The journey was especially hard on the elders and the children.

The Cherokee Trail of Tears

UNITED STATES

OKLAHOMA

SOUTH
CAROLINA

GEORGIA

ALABAMA

MISSISSIPPI

Gulf of Mexico

Legend

Land granted to Cherokees

⟵ Trail Route

Because the journey was so difficult, it became known as the Trail of Tears. Those who survived the Trail of Tears had another battle to face. They had to settle into their new homeland, in what later would become the state of Oklahoma. In 1839, the Cherokee wrote a constitution to create their own government. During the late 1800s, Cherokees set up farms, opened schools, and continued publishing a newspaper called the *Cherokee Advocate*. The rebuilding of the Cherokee Nation had begun.

The Cherokee suffered terribly on their long journey from the Appalachians to the plains of Oklahoma. The long trip became known as the Trail of Tears.

Sequoyah

In 1821, a Cherokee man named Sequoyah completed a written form of the Cherokee language. It was not an alphabet, but was called a syllabary. The syllabary contains pronunciations as well as letters. He wanted his people to be able to read and write in Cherokee as he saw the white explorers and settlers read and write in English.

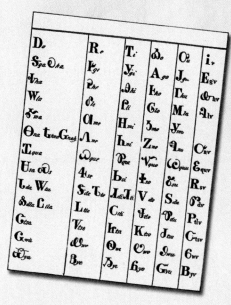

Seqouyah was in the U.S. Army during the War of 1812 (1812–1814). He wanted to be able to write home to his family using his own language. Until this time, the Cherokee language had only been spoken. There were no written Cherokee documents.

Sequoyah created a syllabary made up of 85 characters. Each character represented a syllable from the Cherokee language. The Cherokee still use this syllabary today. Sequoyah served the Cherokee people as a statesman until his death.

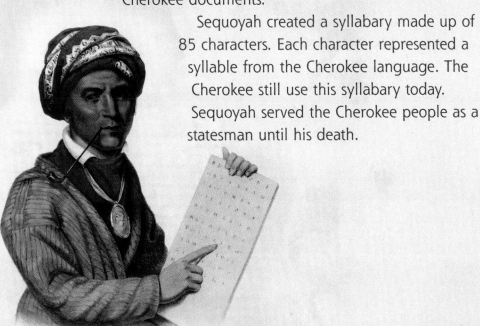

This group of Cherokee is performing the Stomp Dance. Cherokee learn about their culture and heritage from family and elders as well as at the schools they attend.

Chapter Four

Life in a Modern World

Cherokee live throughout the United States, but most live in cities and towns in Oklahoma and North Carolina. Like many other American children, Cherokee children ride the bus to school, play computer and video games, and send e-mail to their friends. They also might attend Stomp Dances, listen to Cherokee legends, and learn to read and write in their native Cherokee language.

Education

With the development of a written language in the early 1800s, many Cherokee children learned to read and write. Schools continue to teach the Cherokee language through Cherokee teachers and by the use of special computer software. There are many dialects in the Cherokee language.

Cherokee schools are modern and have all the latest equipment.

Chadwick Smith

Chadwick "Corntassel" Smith is the Principal Chief of the Cherokee Nation. The people elected him in 1999. A deputy chief and a 15-member council aid Smith. The chief and council oversee the development of social programs, such as good-quality health care and education.

Smith has worked most of his life in the service of the Cherokee people. As a practicing attorney, he donated much of his time helping elders, children, and families. Smith respects and understands the needs of the Cherokee people. He understands how important it is to listen to the people, encourage participation, and get tribal members into the government.

His vision for the Cherokee nation puts emphasis on education and health care. He is working to ensure the promotion and preservation of the culture, heritage, traditions, and language of the Cherokee people.

A dialect is the way a language is spoken among a particular group of people. Overhill, Upper, Middle, and Lower are the most common dialects. Most people today speak the Overhill dialect. Children learn the different dialects in school.

Wilma Mankiller

Wilma Mankiller served as Principal Chief of the Cherokee Nation from 1985 to 1995. She was officially elected to the position in 1987. Mankiller was the first woman chief of the Cherokee Nation.

When Mankiller was born in 1945, she was the sixth of 11 children. They lived on a farm in Oklahoma. The living conditions were very poor. Mankiller's family did not have running water or electricity.

In 1981, Mankiller began working on community projects. She successfully organized a program that equipped 110 families in an Oklahoma town with running water. Following this project and other successful projects, Mankiller went on to become Principal Chief of the Cherokee Nation.

The Cherokee place a great importance on education. They have built many new schools. Cherokees set up excellent school systems. They provide their children with the latest technologies and software. Many Cherokee students go on to attend college or vocational training.

Economics

The Cherokee people work in many different professions. Some are doctors, lawyers, teachers, farmers, miners, factory workers, or artists. Cherokee people can get the training and education they need to get good paying jobs.

The Cherokee have opened several bingo facilities in Oklahoma. The money they make funds a variety of services, including education and health services. The nation also owns several other businesses and factories.

Health Care and Politics

The Cherokee have a good health care program, including up-to-date clinics and hospitals. The U.S. Public Health Service runs most health programs. The Cherokee learn about healthy living and disease prevention at local clinics and community centers.

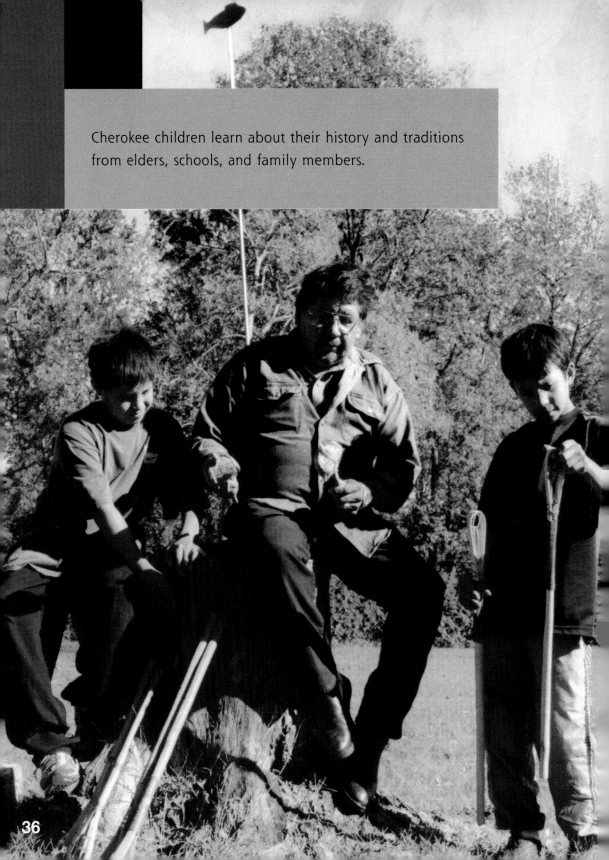

Cherokee children learn about their history and traditions from elders, schools, and family members.

Chapter Five

Sharing the Old Ways

Cherokee children have the opportunity to learn about their culture and history in schools and from their elders. Children also gather with family and friends to attend traditional cultural events, such as Stomp Dances and feasts. Children can learn about their history from the Cherokee Heritage Center in Oklahoma and the Oconaluftee Indian Village in North Carolina.

Cherokee teach their children about their heritage through stories that have moral and cultural values. This picture, *At the Pool of Creation*, is a representation of a creation story.

Elders

Cherokee children learn about morals and cultural values by listening to their elders. They also learn about their tribe's history through stories. Elders tell stories at cultural events, such as dances and ceremonies. Grandparents, aunts, and uncles tell stories to the children in their families.

Cherokee elders also pass on their heritage through art and books. People can learn about other Cherokee experiences by reading their books and looking at their paintings and artwork.

Legend of the Universe

The Cherokee have many different legends. One of them is the story of the universe. This legend has been handed down from generation to generation. Today's elders continue to pass this story down to the children. The Cherokee used to believe that the world was made up of three separate worlds. There was the Upper World, the Lower World, and This World.

This World was a round island resting on the surface of the water. Four cords from each of the directions of the compass attached it to the sky. Each direction had its own color that represented something from the Lower World or the Upper World. The Upper World had perfect order and stability. The Lower World was full of disorder.

East was the color red, because it was the color of the sun. Red was also the color of fire and represented life. North was the direction of cold, so its color was blue. It represented trouble and defeat. South was the direction of warmth, and its color was white. It was associated with peace and happiness. The moon was in the west. It gave no warmth and unlike the Sun, it was not a giver of life. Black was the color that represented the west. The west stood for death and the souls of the dead.

The Cherokee believed that it was their role to find a halfway spot between the Upper World and the Lower World. This spot should be found while living in This World.

Museums and Cultural Events

Many large cities with high populations of Cherokee people have gathering places. In Tahlequah, Oklahoma, visitors can see the Cherokee Heritage Center. Here, people can learn about Cherokee history and culture. Elders come to the center to teach classes about crafts or language. Both young and old people gather to share their stories and experiences.

At the Cherokee Heritage Center, people can see how Cherokee lived in centuries past. They can watch demonstrations of Cherokee crafts and skills.

At the Cherokee Heritage Center in Oklahoma, visitors can walk through the Ancient Village. They can see how Cherokee lived in centuries past. They can watch demonstrations of Cherokee crafts and skills.

Eastern Cherokee of North Carolina teach their children and visitors about their history and culture in a play called *Unto These Hills*. They perform this play outdoors during the summer months.

In 1952, the Eastern Cherokee opened the Oconaluftee Indian Village. This collection of Cherokee houses, crafts, and clothing shows what a village looked like 200 years ago.

In Tennessee, people can visit the Sequoyah Birthplace Museum. This museum is the only one in Tennessee the Cherokee own. People can learn about Sequoyah's creation of the Cherokee syllabary and about his life. Each September, visitors can attend the Cherokee Arts and Crafts festival on the museum's grounds.

In Oklahoma, the Cherokee Nation offers many events that teach others about Cherokee history and culture. Traditional Stomp Dances are held monthly. In September, the Cherokee celebrate the Cherokee National Holidays that were established in 1957. Families enjoy dances, feasts, and ceremonies.

Unto These Hills is a play that Cherokee perform outdoors during the summer months. The play tells about Cherokee history.

Cherokee Timeline

English settlers begin to trade with the Cherokee.

Sequoyah completes the Cherokee syllabary.

1540   1620   1754   1821

Hernando de Soto and his soldiers have the first contact with the Cherokee.

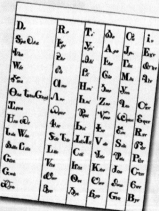

France and Great Britain went to war in 1754. In North America this conflict became known as the French and Indian War (1754–1763).

The U.S. government forces the Cherokee to leave their homelands. The Trail of Tears is the journey in which more than 4000 people die.

Wilma Mankiller is the first woman elected to become Principal Chief.

1838-1839   **1957**   **1987**   **1999**

Chadwick "Corntassel" Smith is elected Principal Chief of the Cherokee Nation.

The first Cherokee National Holiday is announced.

Glossary

ancestors (AN-sess-tur)—family members that lived a long time ago

measles (MEE-zuhlz)—an infectious disease causing fever and rash

nation (NAY-shuhn)—another word for tribe, or a group of people who live in the same area, speak the same language, and follow the same chief

sacred (SAY-krid)—highly valued, and important

smallpox (SMAWL-poks)—a contagious disease that causes chills and high fevers and leads to death

treaty (TREE-tee)—a legal agreement between nations

tribe (TRIBE)—a group of people who live in the same area, speak the same language, and follow the same chief

For Further Reading

Bial, Raymond. *The Cherokee.* Lifeways Series. New York: Benchmark Books, 1999.

Bruchac, Joseph. *The Trail of Tears.* Step into Reading. New York: Random House, 1999.

McClure, Tony Mack. *Cherokee Proud: A Guide for Tracing and Honoring Your Cherokee Ancestors.* Somerville, Tenn: Chunannee Books, 1999.

Sneve, Virginia Driving Hawk. *The Cherokees.* A First Americans Book. New York: Holiday House, 1996.

Places to Write & Visit

Cherokee Heritage Center
P.O. Box 515
Tahlequah, OK 74465-0515

Cherokee Historical Association
P.O. Box 398
US Highway 441 North
Cherokee, NC 28719

National Trail of Tears Association
1100 North University, Suite 143
Little Rock, AR 72207-6344

Internet Sites

Track down many sites about the Cherokee.
Visit the FactHound at http://www.facthound.com

IT IS EASY! IT IS FUN!

1) Go to *http://www.facthound.com*
2) Type in: 0736813551
3) Click on "FETCH IT" and FactHound
   will find several links hand-picked
   by our editors.

**Relax and let our pal FactHound do
the research for you!**

Index